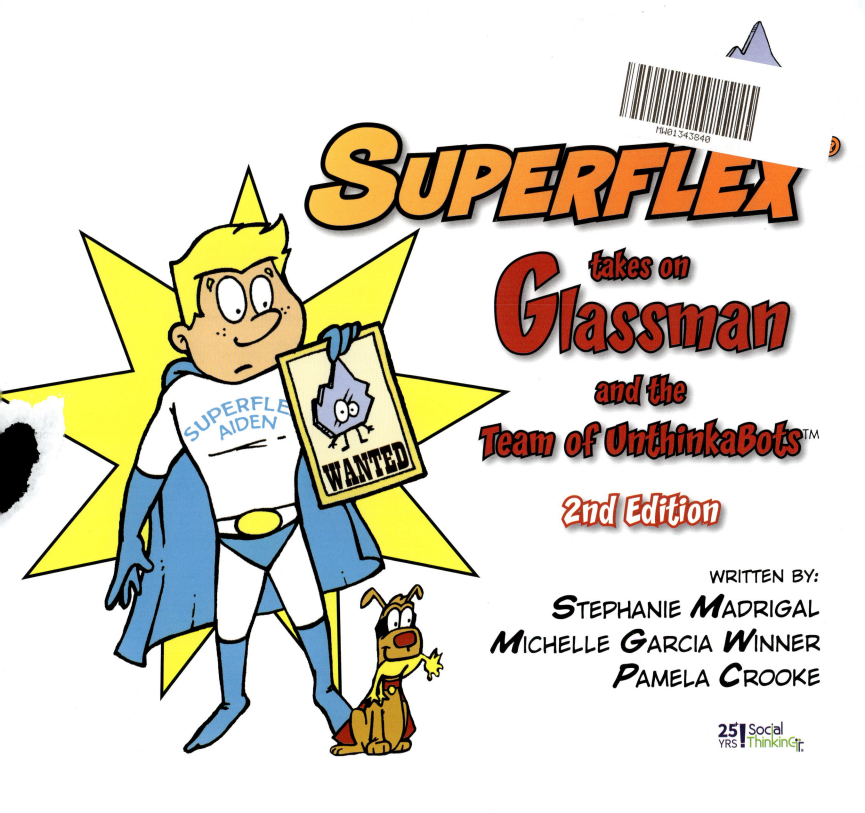

Superflex® takes on Glassman and the Team of UnthinkaBots™, 2nd Edition

Stephanie Madrigal, Michelle Garcia Winner, and Pamela Crooke

Copyright © 2022, 2009 Think Social Publishing, Inc.

All Rights Reserved except as noted herein.

NOTE: The Social Thinking Methodology is made up of language-based curricula, frameworks, and strategies. Because our methodology is dynamic, the language we use to teach evolves along with the culture at large combined with the feedback we get directly from our clients and community. This volume replaces the term Unthinkable with UnthinkaBot and includes minimal but important updates to descriptive language and character artwork to teach basic concepts.

Outside of the specific use described below, all other reproduction/copying, adaptation, conversion to electronic format, or sharing/distribution of content, through print or electronic means, is not permitted without written permission from Think Social Publishing, Inc. (TSP).

This includes prohibition of any use of any content or materials from this product as part of an adaptation or derivative work you create for posting on a personal or business website, TeachersPayTeachers, YouTube, Pinterest, Facebook, or any other social media or information sharing site in existence now or in the future, whether free or for a fee. Exceptions are made, upon written request, for product reviews, articles, and blogposts.

TSP grants permission to the owner of this book to use and/or adapt content in print or electronic form, only for direct in-classroom/school/home or in-clinic use with your own students/clients/children, and with the primary stakeholders in that individual's life, which includes parents, caregivers and direct service personnel. The copyright for any adaptation of content owned by TSP remains with TSP as a derivative work.

Social Thinking, Superflex, The Unthinkables, The UnthinkaBots, The Thinkables, and We Thinkers! GPS are trademarks belonging to TSP.

Translation of this product can only be done in accordance with our TRANSLATION POLICY found on our intellectual property website page here: https://www.socialthinking.com/intellectual-property.

And, visit our intellectual property page to find detailed TERMS OF USE information and a DECISION-TREE that cover copyright, trademark, and intellectual property topics and questions governing the use of our materials.

ISBN: 978-1-936943-93-7 (print)

Think Social Publishing, Inc.
404 Saratoga Avenue, Suite 200
Santa Clara, CA 95050
Tel: (408) 557-8595
Fax: (408) 557-8594

Illustrated by Kelly Knopp

This book was printed and bound in the United States by Mighty Color Printing.
TSP is a sole source provider of Social Thinking products in the U.S.
Books may be purchased online at www.socialthinking.com

This illustrated story book is dedicated to all the professionals, caregivers, and students who have helped develop Superflex, the Unthinkables/UnthinkaBots, and the Superflex Academy.

All children can benefit from the social emotional teaching that is at the foundation of the Social Thinking Methodology. The Superflex series, including this storybook, is for both neurotypical and Neurodivergent students who have solid language and academic learning. The book can be used in the classroom, small group settings, 1:1 teaching, or at home.

Recommended Teaching & Learning Pathway for using the Superflex Series

3-Step Pathway for kids ages 5-10*

1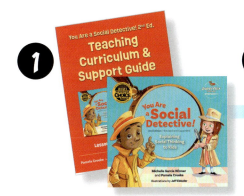

Use the *You Are a Social Detective!* 2nd Ed. storybook and Teaching Curriculum first to introduce key Social Thinking concepts/Vocabulary to build social awareness.

2

After building social awareness and a social vocabulary, depending on the age of your student, introduce Superflex to teach about self-regulation toward behavior change.

3

Use any other Superflex books, games, and visuals AFTER teaching the Superflex Curriculum to take learning to a deeper level.

If you're working with kids ages 9-12

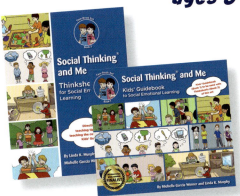

Start with Social Detective.

Next, *Social Thinking and Me* is used BEFORE or alongside teaching the Superflex Curriculum.

This two-book set helps deepen students' understanding of core Social Thinking concepts and gives them lots of practice to build stronger social competencies.

For kids aging out of Superflex (age 10+)

Start with *Social Thinking and Me* (if not already taught).

Next, move on to *Social Fortune or Social Fate*. (ages 10+)

* Some younger kids with social learning differences may need more time building their Social Detective skills. Wait to start Superflex with them until around age 8.

Find articles about teaching Superflex plus other books and teaching materials at www.SocialThinking.com

One Step at a Time!

Cautions and Information About the Use of This Material

Superflex takes on Glassman and the Team of UnthinkaBots is a storybook in our Superflex series designed to help children learn more about their own social behavior and strategies to regulate it. As charming and captivating as Superflex and the Team of UnthinkaBots are to students, this is ***not*** a starting place for teaching. Social Thinking Vocabulary and related concepts need to be introduced first to help children explore what it means to think social, to learn to be social observers and problem solvers, and understand the relationship between social thoughts and social behavioral expectations for the situation.

To be used effectively, parents and educators need to start at the beginning, introduce core concepts, and work through the Superflex Curriculum ***before*** sharing this storybook (or others to follow) with children. Books should be introduced in this order (see note if working with older kids):

1. *You Are a Social Detective!* 2nd Edition storybook and the companion *You Are a Social Detective! 2nd Ed. Teaching Curriculum and Support Guide*
2. *Superflex...A Superhero Social Thinking® Curriculum* that includes the book *Superflex takes on Rock Brain and the Team of Unthinkables*

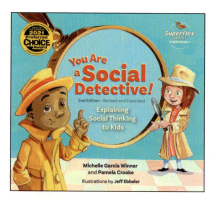

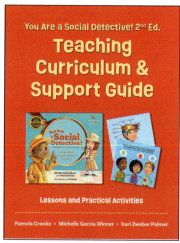

Once these books have been introduced, adults are free to move on to any of the individual UnthinkaBots books, games, music, or visual supports we have produced to date, in any order that meets the child's social learning differences or interests.

In *You Are a Social Detective!*, 2nd Ed., children are introduced – through child-friendly illustrations and language - to core concepts that make up the Social Thinking® Methodology. Use the companion *You Are a Social Detective! 2nd Ed. Teaching Curriculum & Support Guide*, an easy-to-use

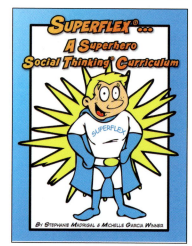

curriculum that fits into your current teaching day. The storybook introduces students to core social emotional learning (SEL) concepts, and the curriculum provides 10 fun, structured lesson plans and visual tools to support building students' social attention, social interpretation, and self-awareness—the foundation for social emotional learning for everyone.

Superflex...A Superhero Social Thinking® Curriculum introduces Superflex Aiden. He is a boy who learns to transform himself into a superhero to help the citizens of Social Town outsmart the Team of UnthinkaBots. Fun exercises motivate students to learn more about how their brain works; concrete strategies give them tools to become better social observers and social problem solvers.

In *Superflex Takes on Rock Brain and the Team of UnthinkaBots*, children are exposed to their first UnthinkaBot character as they work through the Superflex Curriculum. This foundation of learning sets the stage for them to then move on to other books in the series. Each storybook highlights a particular UnthinkaBot and its powers while teaching readers about strategies they can use to manage their own UnthinkaBots.

Adults can learn more about the Social Thinking Methodology in the book *Why Teach Social Thinking?* (Winner, 2013). Many free articles, webinars, and information about additional resources can be found at www.socialthinking.com.

Note: If you're teaching Superflex in a general education classroom, or starting Superflex with kids who are a little older, we suggest adding another book into the teaching series: *Social Thinking and Me*. This two-book set, aimed at kids ages 9-12, takes a deeper look into core Social Thinking concepts and helps kids get the practice they need to integrate this new information into everyday activities. See the Learning Pathways page for when to introduce it into the teaching series.

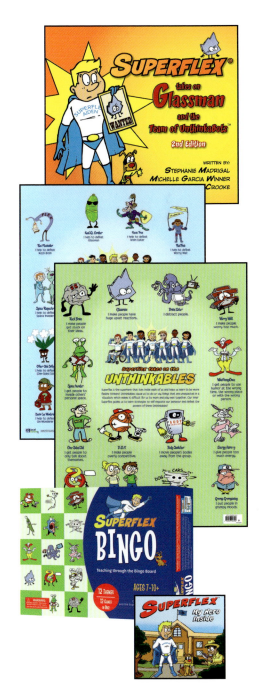

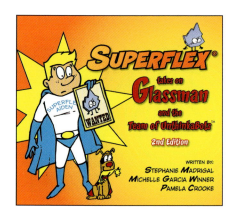

About This Book
In *Superflex Takes on Glassman and the Team of UnthinkaBots*, children become familiar with some social learning strategies they can use to help them manage Glassman's (aka Glassy) powers to challenge their thinking and make them have huge reactions, even to small problems. Although the story introduces specific strategies, not all strategies presented in the book will apply to every child. Caregivers and educators should closely evaluate what strategies are a match for each child and encourage them to identify what strategies they do and don't like.

Additional Social Thinking resources related to problem solving strategies:
- *Superflex and Kool Q. Cumber to the Rescue!*
- *We Thinkers!* series (Volume 2, Unit 9, *Size of the Problem*)
- The Zones of Regulation™ series

Using the Series: Things to Keep in Mind
- Children who will benefit from the Superflex curriculum are those who can differentiate well between fantasy and reality. They are encouraged to think about and understand that Superflex is a pretend character, and should be able to imagine they can pretend to transform themselves into their own superflexible superhero and use their own strategies for problem solving. This is a very different concept than pretending to be a superhero in a play situation. Pre-teach children that managing an UnthinkaBot is something that happens in their brains and is not a battle with their bodies. Children who struggle with these ideas may not be good candidates for and of the books in the Superflex series.

- The concepts in this book are best suited for students ages 8-11 with social learning differences. While many neurotypical students ages 5-7 will also find this material engaging and helpful, students of that age with social learning differences may find it too demanding too soon in their social learning lives!

- If students protest or don't enjoy this idea of superheroes, then please discontinue using this curriculum as a teaching tool and spend more time helping those children learn about the social world that surrounds them. Not every child is ready to take on his or her own personal program for behavior self-regulation.

- The ultimate goal is to help children become better observers of social information and improve their responses and related social skills.

Congratulations! If you are reading this story, you've probably been picked to be a student at the Superflex Academy. At the Academy, you will learn how to become your own Superflex, a special kind of superhero.

You will study the sneaky ways of the *Team of UnthinkaBots*, who would like to get into the thinking inside your brain and get you to do or say things that show you aren't thinking about others. In this book you will learn from a Thinkable character, Kool Q. Cumber, who will give Aiden some ideas about how to manage Glassman (Glassy).

Part of your Superflex training is to get to know each and every one of these UnthinkaBots – in case you need to work on managing them! Reading this story is one of the many fun things you will get to do while attending the very important Superflex Academy.

Along this adventure there will also be fun Social Town facts and quizzes to show your Superflex smarts. Possible answers can be found on the last pages of the book.

The UnthinkaBots

Body Drifter
I move people's bodies away from the group with DriftBots.

Blurt Out Blue
I get people to call out or blurt with BlurtBots.

Brain Eater
I distract people using DistractoBots.

D.O.F.
I make people overly competitive with CompetiBots.

Energy Hare-y
I give people too much energy with EnergyBots.

Glassman
I make people have huge upset reactions with ExplodaBots.

Mean Bean
I get people to act mean and bossy using MeanBots.

Me-Gull
I get people to only talk about themselves using MeBots.

Rock Brain
I make people get stuck on their ideas with StuckBots.

Space Invader
I get people to invade others' personal space with CloseBots.

Topic Twistermeister
I make people jump off topic with TwistaBots.

Un-Wonderer
I don't let people socially wonder about others using UnwonderBots.

WasFunnyOnce
I get people to use humor at the wrong time, place, and/or with the wrong person using SillyBots.

Worry Wall
I make people worry too much using WorryBots.

The Team of UnthinkaBots has been around a long time, invading the brains of Social Town citizens! In Social Town, people live together and think about each other every day.

In this story, Glassman and others will try their luck at taking over Social Town. All of the UnthinkaBots are pretty clever, and sometimes find ways to combine their powers.

You will see UnthinkaBots lurking in the corners of some pages, just waiting to help Glassman. When you see them, try to imagine what you might do if that UnthinkaBot was in your brain.

You see, each one of us can learn to be a superflexible superhero that looks just like us. Our pets can even become superpets too!

Last summer, the sneaky UnthinkaBots tried
to take over Social Town by hiding the Superflex Brain Sensor.
Luckily, Aiden and Bark found it. When the UnthinkaBots are active, the
Brain Sensor sends out a message for all Superflexes, everywhere, to
transform themselves into their Superflexes.

SUPERFLEXES remember to...

- be flexible thinkers
- use their flexible thinking strategies to manage the UnthinkaBots
- be thinking of many different ways to solve problems
- help other Superflexes when UnthinkaBots are near

THE UNTHINKABOT: GLASSMAN

Glassman has visited the brains of almost all of us, even parents and teachers. Glassman, or Glassy, has a way of making our brains think that every single problem is a HUGE problem. But we all know that problems come in all sizes. Glassman makes us want to always react in a HUGE way, even with little problems.

Glassman is shaped like broken glass because when things don't go our way, Glassy sends ExplodaBots to get our thinking and actions to shatter like a pane of glass.

Glassman, or Glassy, is one of the most common UnthinkaBots. That makes sense. Remember: most of us (even grownups) have had Glassman's ExplodaBots in our brains before. But don't worry, this book is going to give you some choices for how to manage this character if you notice it in your brain.

Activity Alert!

Draw a picture of what you think Glassman's ExplodaBots look like.

Aiden couldn't wait for the school year to begin. He wanted to tell the kids at school about how he and Bark found the Superflex Brain Sensor over the summer break. And, he wanted to tell them how he learned to transform himself into Superflex Aiden and how they could learn too.

Today, Social Town citizens are thinking of one another. But, last summer, Glassman was in the brains of many Social Town kids...

Superflex Quiz #1:

Have you ever had a "Glassman moment" and had a huge negative reaction to something that others thought was a tiny problem?

Over the summer, Aiden's mom made a special meeting with the principal and Aiden's teacher to make sure everyone knew about Aiden's new Superflex powers.

Everyone agreed to make a plan for Aiden to leave class if the Brain Sensor went off. Mrs. Cruz and Aiden decided on a special signal: Aiden would raise his hand and look down at his backpack that had the Brain Sensor and his Superflex costume.

Are these tiny problems?
Let's check the size of the problem!

What is the size of my problem?

1. Think about a problem and rank it on a scale of 1-10.

   Losing a game at recess is a huge 10!

2. To check if that's true, think of a really BIG problem.

   It was a 10 when I broke my leg.

3. Now compare the two like a math problem.

   Does breaking a leg
   equal (=) or not equal (≠)
   losing a game at recess?

   They don't equal each other. That means losing is a smaller problem.

4. Keep thinking of different problems and their sizes and then compare them on a scale of 1-10.

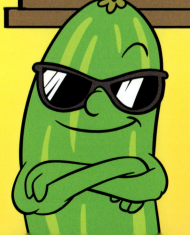

Once you know the size of the problem, you can keep Glassman from making you think it's bigger than it is!

"Now that you know about different sizes of problems, you can learn how to match reactions to three different sized problems."

BIG problems (8-10)

are those that you can't solve without a trusted adult to help. Things like broken bones or a fire or even bullies can be big problems. People often have big reactions like crying or yelling to really big problems. These reactions match the size of the problem so they are not confusing to others.

MEDIUM problems (4-7)

are those that can make people feel worried or stressed, like losing your homework or having a cold. Medium problems can be solved with a little help from others. Sometimes people react to medium problems by worrying or telling others they are upset. These reactions match the size of the problem so they are not confusing to others.

TINY problems (1-3)

are those that we can solve by ourselves, even though Glassman might make the problem seem huge. Tiny problems can be breaking your pencil lead or not being first in line. Reactions to tiny problems are things like sighing, deep breathing, or squeezing your hands together. These reactions match the size of the problem so they are not confusing to others.

Superflex Quiz #3:

Give an example of a big, medium, and tiny problem.

Let's go see what's happening back in Social Town.

Aiden is happy he gets to sit next to his friend Sam and be with one of his favorite teachers, Mrs. Cruz.

Aiden and the other kids notice that Sam looks really angry. Sam pounds his hand on the desk and yells, NOOOOO! Everyone is having confused thoughts.

Take a big breath in and make your body really tight (like a cucumber skin) and then, relax your muscles as you breathe out.

Let's see how this strategy helped out on the playground!

Mrs. Cruz could tell this was going to be a great class.

She saw that the students remembered there are hidden rules in the classroom, not just posted rules. How did she know?

She knew they remembered the hidden rules in the classroom, because all of the kids were listening with their brains and bodies.

Superflex Quiz #4:

"Hidden rules" or "unspoken rules" are not posted on the wall, but we are supposed to figure them out in our brains anyway. For example, one hidden rule is that we use quiet voices when people are sleeping. Another is that we throw our trash in the can and not on the floor. Superflexes can learn how to figure out the hidden rules but UnthinkaBots don't want us to.

Can you think of three hidden rules in the classroom?

Suddenly, Aiden notices the Superflex Brain Sensor is shaking. He remembers that if he needs to leave the class that he has a special signal with Mrs. Cruz. He looks at his backpack and raises his hand and waits for her to notice him.

Aiden and Bark find a corner in the hallway and pull out the Superflex Brain Sensor. In the blink of an eye, they are standing in their awesome Superflex costumes.

The Superflex Brain Sensor shines this message on the wall:

ROCK BRAIN ALERT!
A student in Room 3 is getting stuck because his pencil broke.

GLASSMAN ALERT!
The student is yelling and rolling around on the floor. Others in the classroom are having confused thoughts and are feeling nervous.

We all have a coach in our brains called an "inner coach." This brain coach helps think of positive words (or positive self-talk) to keep us going when we have problems to solve.

But watch out! Glassman, Rock Brain, and the other UnthinkaBots don't like positive self-talk. They want you to use negative self-talk or negative words in your thinking that can make you stuck.

The Superflex Academy students were hard at work using their inner coaches and practicing their positive self-talk strategies they had learned about in class.

Superflex Aiden hands Taylor the Superflex Brain Sensor that projects this Superflex strategy on the wall:

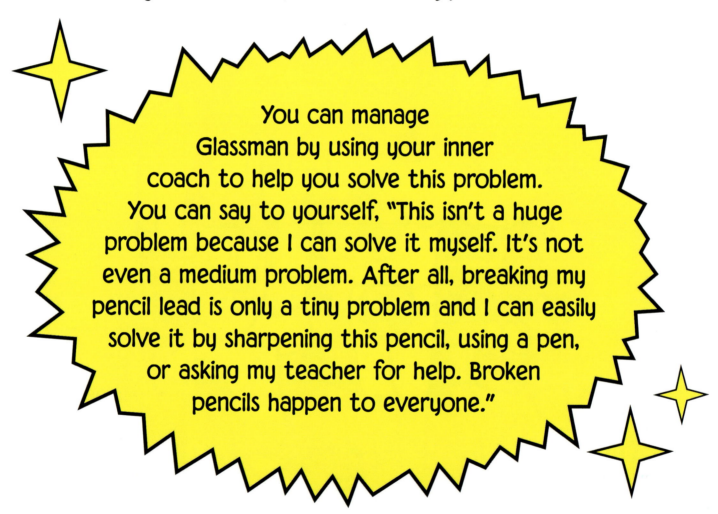

You can manage Glassman by using your inner coach to help you solve this problem. You can say to yourself, "This isn't a huge problem because I can solve it myself. It's not even a medium problem. After all, breaking my pencil lead is only a tiny problem and I can easily solve it by sharpening this pencil, using a pen, or asking my teacher for help. Broken pencils happen to everyone."

Superflex Quiz #6:

List three of your own positive self-talk statements.

Taylor did it! He managed Glassman's ExplodaBots and solved his small problem with Thinkable strategies from Kool Q. Cumber. His classmates are proud to see that Taylor is becoming his own Superflex! They are no longer confused by his reaction and feel good about learning together!

Superflex Quiz #7:

What strategy would you use if this problem happened to you?

UNTHINKABOT & THINKABLE
Character Pairings

Our inner Superflex can work as a team with one or more Thinkables to provide good ideas and strategies to help manage the UnthinkaBots. Below are some common UnthinkaBots you may find around Social Town and their paired Thinkables character counterparts.

UNTHINKABOTS ▼	▼ THINKABLES

Body Drifter
I move people's bodies away from the group with DriftBots.

Stick-Withem
I help you keep your body with the group and your shoulders turned toward the group.

Blurt Out Blue
I get people to call out or blurt with BlurtBots.

Thought Catcher
I help you to be aware of your thoughts and decide which thoughts to turn into words and which thoughts stay in your brain.

Brain Eater
I distract people using DistractoBots.

Focus Tron
I help give you focusing powers so your brain can stay connected to what others are talking about or what you are doing.

D.O.F. (Destroyer of Fun)
I make people overly competitive with CompetiBots.

I.O.F. (Inventor of Fun)
I help you use your positive thinking so you can cooperate and be flexible during sports and games.

UNTHINKABOT & THINKABLE
Character Pairings

UNTHINKABOTS ▼   **▼ THINKABLES**

Energy Hare-y
I give people too much energy with EnergyBots.

Aware Hare
I help you be aware of strategies to use to help calm your body.

Glassman
I make people have huge upset reactions with ExplodaBots.

Kool Q. Cumber
I help you figure out the size of the problem and help you to stay calm (cool as a cucumber) when there are small problems.

Mean Bean
I get people to act mean and bossy using MeanBots.

Nice Light
I help you say nice, friendly words to others even if you don't feel like being friendly.

Me-Gull
I get people to only talk about themselves using MeBots.

We-Gulls
We help you remember that conversations are also about thinking about the other person or persons and finding out about them.

Rock Brain
I make people get stuck on their ideas with StuckBots.

T-Flex
I help you be a flexible thinker so you don't get stuck on your own thoughts or plans.

UNTHINKABOT & THINKABLE
Character Pairings

UNTHINKABOTS ▼			▼ THINKABLES
Space Invader — I get people to invade others' personal space with CloseBots.			**Space Base** — I help you understand your own and other's personal space base bubbles.
Topic Twistermeister — I make people jump off topic with TwistaBots.			**Tracker** — I help you stay on the right track or topic the group is talking about.
Un-Wonderer — I don't let people socially wonder about others using UnwonderBots.			**The Wonderer** — I remind you to think about and use your social wonder questions to learn about others during conversations.
WasFunnyOnce — I get people to use humor at the wrong time, place, and/or with the wrong person using SillyBots.			**Dr. HumorUs** — I help you know the right time, right place, and the right people with whom to use humor.
Worry Wall — I make people worry too much using WorryBots.			**Worry WiseWorm** — I help you figure out when (or if) you should worry. I also help you with ways to manage your worries.

45

Superflex Quiz Answers

There are many correct responses and possible answers to the quizzes you've taken throughout the book, so don't worry if your answers do not match the ones below.

Superflex Quiz #1:

Have you ever had a "Glassman moment" and had a huge negative reaction to something that others thought was a tiny problem?

Possible answers: I might have a huge reaction when my mom makes me go to a restaurant I don't like, when the cafeteria runs out of chocolate milk just before I get up to the front of the line, or when my teacher tells me to put away the book I'm reading.

Superflex Quiz #2:

Which UnthinkaBot is helping Glassman?
Can you think of a Superflex strategy to manage this character?

Possible answer: D.O.F, the Destroyer of Fun, is the UnthinkaBot working with Glassman.

Use positive self-talk and say to yourself: I just want to have fun playing this game – it doesn't matter who wins.

Superflex Quiz #3:

Give an example of a big, medium, and tiny problem.

Possible answers:

Tiny problem: A fly buzzing in my face. My shoe coming untied.

Medium problem: Forgetting my homework. Getting teased.

Big problem: Breaking my ankle. A dog attack. An earthquake.

Superflex Quiz #4:

"Hidden rules" or "unspoken rules" are not posted on the wall, but we are supposed to figure them out in our brains anyway. For example, one hidden rule is that we use quiet voices when people are sleeping. Another is that we throw our trash in the can and not on the floor. Superflexes can learn how to figure out the hidden rules but UnthinkaBots don't want us to.

Can you think of three hidden rules in the classroom?

Possible hidden rules in the classroom:
Students take turns talking in class by raising their hand and waiting.
Students figure out how to listen with their brains and bodies.
If the lesson is boring, students keep that thought inside their head.

Superflex Quiz #5:

Can you make guesses about what the students in the class are thinking and feeling?

Possible guesses:

Thinking: What is wrong? That is a tiny problem. I don't want to sit by him.

Feeling: Confused. Worried. Stressed.

Superflex Quiz #6:

List three of your own positive self-talk statements.

Possible self-talk statements:
1. This is a tiny problem, so my tiny reaction is to take a deep breath and think about my choices.
2. I can always ask my teacher for help if the work gets too hard.
3. I can take some deep breaths. This always helps me stay calm.

Superflex Quiz #7:

What strategy would you use if this problem happened to you?

Possible answer: I would ask my classmate sitting next to me if I could borrow a pencil.

Thinkables to the Rescue!

AVAILABLE NOW!

- Companion books to the *Brain Eater* and *Glassman* illustrated storybooks
- Help children compare and contrast the inner workings of their brain in tackling everyday social challenges
- Celebrate their ability to manage UnthinkaBots when they appear
- Use the Thinkables as positive character substitutes to shift attention in situations where students find it fun to act out only the negative powers of the UnthinkaBots

Preview pages from each Thinkable book and learn how to use these companion tools on their respective product pages on our website **www.socialthinking.com**.

The Superflex® Series
Curriculum, storybooks, visual supports, tools, and games

Books

Posters

Music

Games

Stickers

Read hundreds of free articles on our website, including:
- Superflex® Teaches Super Metacognitive Strategies
- 10 DOs and DON'Ts for Teaching Superflex

Check out our On Demand Series on Superflex:
- Social Detective, Superflex®, and Friends Take on Social Emotional Learning

To learn more, visit www.socialthinking.com

SocialThinking has so much to offer!

OUR MISSION

At Social Thinking, our mission is to help people develop social competencies to better connect with others and experience deeper well-being. We create unique teaching frameworks and strategies to help individuals develop their social thinking and social emotional learning to meet their academic, personal and professional social goals. These goals often include sharing space effectively with others, learning to work as part of a team, and developing relationships of all kinds: with family, friends, classmates, co-workers, romantic partners, etc.

FREE ARTICLES & WEBINARS

100+ free educational articles and webinars about our teaching strategies

LIVESTREAM EVENTS, ON DEMAND COURSES & CUSTOM TRAINING

Live and recorded trainings for schools and organizations

PRODUCTS

Print and ebooks, games, decks, posters, music and more!

CLINICAL RESEARCH

Measuring the effectiveness of the Social Thinking® Methodology

SERVICES: CHILDREN & ADULTS

Clinical services, assessments, school consultations, etc.

CLINICAL TRAINING PROGRAM

Three-day intensive training for professionals

www.socialthinking.com